Darkest Hour
the

A Comprehensive Account of the Smith Mine Disaster of 1943

the Darkest Hour
A Comprehensive Account of the Smith Mine Disaster of 1943

3rd Edition

1st edition by Fay Kuhlman
2nd/3rd editions by Gary D. Robson

Proseyr Publishing
Red Lodge, MT U.S.A.

Copyright ©2003-2011 Gary Robson
and the Carbon County Historical Society

All rights reserved.

The Darkest Hour
By Fay Kuhlman and Gary D. Robson

Body copy set in Book Antiqua
Headings set in Myriad Pro

Cover photo by Gary D. Robson

Third edition
ISBN 978-0-9659609-4-6 (paperback)
ISBN 978-0-9659609-2-2 (ebook)

Proseyr Publishing
PO Box 1630, Red Lodge, MT 59068
www.proseyr.com

Dedicated to the families of those who died in the Smith Mine disaster, many of whom this writer came to know and learned to love; and to the valiant men of the rescue crews who risked everything to do a bad job well.

— Fay Kuhlman (from the 1st edition)

Dedicated to Fay Kuhlman, the co-author I never had a chance to meet. I hope that you would have approved of the way I've brought your work back into print, and the additions that I've made to it.

— Gary Robson (from the 2nd/3rd editions)

Front page of the Friday, March 5, 1943 Carbon County News

The Darkest Hour

Contents

Introduction to the 3rd Edition 2
Foreword 3
The Disaster Site 4
Mining in the 1940's 4
The People of Bearcreek Valley 5
The Morning Was Serene 7
Even "Brownie" Was There 8
Premonition? 9
Number Three 10
First Came the Wind 11
The Power of the Explosion 12
The Influx of Help 13
Side by Side .14
Help For the Living 18
The Grim Night Caravans 20
The Remarkable Families 22
"Soldiers on the Home Front" 22
The Aftermath 23
Placing the Blame 23
The 74 Who Died 26
The Children Speak 28
Three Alive .28
Into Hell and Back 30
The Worst Coal Mining Disasters 31
Epilogue 34

Introduction to the 3rd Edition

What it is that draws people to the story of the explosion in the Smith Mine in 1943? It isn't the worst mining disaster in the country. It isn't even in the top 25. There's much more to the story then the number of people who died.

Since the day that 74 people died in the Smith Mine, there have only been four coal mining disasters in the country with higher death tolls: two in Indiana and two in West Virginia. It's been over 30 years since a mining disaster has claimed as many lives as the Smith Mine explosion (a dam failure at the Buffalo Mining Company coal operation in Saunders, WV killed 125 people the day before the 29th anniversary of the Smith Mine explosion). The event was a major factor contributing to the collapse of the local economy and the near extinction of several nearby communities.

I first discovered Fay Kuhlman's booklet on the Smith Mine disaster in 2001 when someone came into my bookstore looking for a copy. I procured a copy for myself at the same time. After reading it, I remember telling my wife, "Anyone who can read this story without tears in their eyes just isn't human."

The Darkest Hour went out of print shortly thereafter, and it was many months later that the Carbon County Historical Society told me that they had acquired the copyright. I offered to revise, edit, and typeset Fay's work, and the booklet you're holding is the result.

The 2nd edition was released on the 60th anniversary of the explosion in the Smith Mine. The 3rd edition was released in 2011, with relatively minor updates.

In bringing *The Darkest Hour* back into print, I've tried to maintain the flavor of Fay's original tale of the disaster itself while adding more background information and extending the story. I've edited some of her words, but removed none of them. She simply told the tale too well for me to change it.

Foreword

Many reports have been made of the Smith Mine Disaster of February 27, 1943. It was an event that shocked the State of Montana with the worst tragedy in its long history of coal mining. The calamity had far-reaching effects on thousands, and repercussions on communities and towns which came close to bringing them to extinction. Because it was a vital portion of history, this work has been compiled from many sources to provide as comprehensive a record of that time as possible.

The reader must know something of the community of Bearcreek and its people if he is to understand, even in part, the tragedy and pathos, the heroism and glory, of those involved in this event.

The story can best be told by those most affected — the families, neighbors, co-workers and friends of the men who died in that underground blast. The small mimeographed publication of the Bearcreek School, "Bear Facts," also provided considerable coverage of the tragedy by the children of the victims. Court records were probed and newspapers searched. Rescue workers shared many incidents too deeply cut in memory ever to be erased, and still we know much, much, more could be said.

The Disaster Site

The lonely stretch of road in southern Montana between Belfry and Red Lodge—now known as State Highway 308—was a hive of activity in the early 1900s. About 3,000 people lived in the valley around Bearcreek. Bearcreek's current population is under 100, making it Montana's smallest incorporated town. Of the surrounding communities of Scotch Coulee, Stringtown, New Caledonia, Chickentown and International, only a few scattered houses remain today. Washoe, where Smith Mine #3 was actually located, survives as a cluster of homes and a quilt shop.

With some of the highest-quality bituminous coal in Montana, mining was the industry that built the area. A study from the Bureau of Mine Reclamation showed that 98 coal mines operated in Carbon County at one time or another. When coal mining began in the valley around Bearcreek and Washoe in 1900, the mining companies had to haul their coal up the steep hill to Red Lodge, which significantly affected the price of the product.

The Montana, Wyoming, and Southern Railroads built a line to the valley in 1906, which was soon taking out 100 railcars full of coal every day. This total declined in the late 1920's and 1930's as the use of diesel and gasoline as fuel increased, but the area saw somewhat of a resurgence in coal mining in the early 1940's, as more coal was needed for the war efforts.

Mining in the 1940's

Mining was a big industry in the United States then. In 1942, there were 530,861 coal miners in the country, according to the Mine Safety and Health Administration. Accidents and even deaths happened in the coal mines, just as in any other industry. In that same year, there were 1,471 coal mining fatalities (again using MSHA's numbers), representing a bit over one quarter of a percent fatality rate.

The majority of these fatalities were individual accidents, with less than 10% of the deaths attributed to what the National Institute for Occupational Safety and Health (NIOSH) refers to as "mining disasters," where five or more workers die in a single incident.

In February of 1943, the worst coal mining catastrophe in Montana history struck Washoe. Only once in the preceding ten years had so many men died in one coal mining incident (the Pond Creek Mine in Bartley, West Virginia).

The People of Bearcreek Valley

The town of Bearcreek nestles in a valley at the foot of the Rocky Mountains where surrounding hills furnish a vast, natural playground for active children. Its name comes from the bears that used to forage there for berries. The view reaches up to heights that catch the first glimmer of morning sun on lofty palisades and snow-crested peaks and ridges. Its surface soils lend readily to growing gardens, flowers and fruits.

The Bearcreek post office opened on November 22, 1905 with Sarah Criger as its postmaster, and the town was incorporated in 1906 when the Montana, Wyoming & Southern Railroad pulled in. Washoe was the only other Bearcreek Valley town to have a post office of its own. The Washoe post office opened with Earle E. Lombard as its postmaster December 2, 1907, and closed half a century later (July 31, 1959) when the town became too small to sustain its own post office.

The valley was full of people drawn by the rich coal deposits nearby. Its people during the first half of the 20th century were a melting pot of nationalities: a vigorous lot who worked hard and played equally hard. A tremendous sense of humor lightened their heavy work, making the hardships bearable. Rough jokes and horseplay gave vent to a healthy exuberance and grudges seldom lasted beyond the first heated scuffle of flashing tempers. Though quick to fight among themselves with many a bloodied nose and blackened eye, there were just as quickly united into one formidable force against troublemakers from outside.

Their loyalty to community lasted from generation to generation, and became a tradition that mystified newcomers of a later date who saw only the physical scene, the outer scars and the rubble of "ghost town" dimension which followed in the wake of the disaster. Newcomers had no way of knowing a people whose men labored willingly in deep tunnels underground, and came out at the end of a long shift with enough energy and mischief to slam a piece of pie into the face of a fellow worker as he emerged form underground. Outsiders find it hard to understand coal-blackened men who broke icicles from eaves of the washhouses on their way in, to ram against the hot skin of a fellow worker ahead in the shower.

It was a rugged way of life with give and take, but there was always a gentle hand to help whenever it was needed.

The women took pride in their children and their homes, and they suffered much. Just how much, even they soon forgot, for the spirit of the people who made Bearcreek was conditioned to the hard life, and quite effectively rose above it. Their spirit lived strongly beyond the individuals themselves to be felt in the valley by the perceptive, long after most of the miners were gone, providing a link toward understanding the people whose lives and deaths make this story, and who made of Bearcreek a name to be cherished by all who know the place and its true meaning.

Books could be written about the youngsters who grew out of such a setting, reared by parents who taught them to appreciate the unlimited advantages open to them in this great new land, and who gave them a heritage of mental and physical stamina to pursue those opportunities. The world has been greatly enriched by this one community through the high caliber of professional and business people, and the splendid, self-respecting citizens who grew out of it.

The Morning Was Serene

Snow was deep and skies were clear that morning of February 27, 1943, in Washoe. The temperature was mild enough that men off-shift dressed in ordinary "clean-up" clothes to go to the mine office after their paychecks. They talked of many things, for it was a time of national stress during World War II. The *Carbon County News* was full of items about local boys in the armed services. Wartime rationing was in force. Captain Eddie Rickenbacker had appealed to labor unions to cease disruptive strife and make sacrifices along with the rest while the country was fighting for its very life. The winter followed a summer of Victory Gardens, fund drives for the Red Cross, and the people of Bearcreek were very much aware of the state of the nation and the world. Many of them still had family ties in the war-torn "old countries" as well as sons on the battlefields.

It was not only payday at the #3 Smith Mine of the Montana Coal and Iron Company. It was also "time-and-a-half" day for the men who went to work in the tunnels at 8:00 A.M. Though they may have preferred doing something else on their weekend, this extra pay was something they were reluctant to miss, and few of them did.

For Pete Giovetti, operator of a 20-ton motor in the mine, this would be his last trip down. The farm for which he and his family had worked and dreamed was finally bought. After one more day in the mine, their move to the farm would begin. The Giovetti family was in a happy mood.

Clarence Williams had been ill. Very much against his wife's wishes, he insisted on going to work anyway. "I can't miss a time-and-a-half day," he told her.

"Can't you let the work go for this one day and rest until you're feeling better?"

"Tomorrow is Sunday," he answered. "I'll rest then."

Bill Pelo had a flat tire and his partner, Vid Zaputil, waiting at the mine entrance, said to those around him, "If Bill doesn't get here pretty soon, we'll miss our trip down."

But Bill got there, and both of them went on down.

John Hodnik in Scotch Coulee had overslept. He gulped his breakfast and ran all the way down the hill to get there on time.

John Sudar seemed more jovial than usual, his wife recalled later. "While I was getting breakfast for him that morning, he looked at me with a strange, long, penetrating gaze. I've thought of it many times since."

Even "Brownie" Was There

Seventy-seven men went into the Smith Mine that fateful morning for their time-and-a-half day. All of them saw Brownie at the entrance and knew that Bill Shepard had gone ahead of them. Brownie, the little cocker spaniel, had waited faithfully for the last five years while Bill worked his shifts in the mine. The little dog knew that there'd always be half a sandwich left for him in Bill's lunch pail when his master came out of the mine.

There were many veterans of the slopes in this crew: men who knew their work and knew the mine. Many were considered among the best mining men in the state. Elmer Price knew every nook and cranny in the mine. David Murray, the foreman, had spent most of his life working for Smith. He knew production. The Mourich brothers, Frank and Jack, could do anything with electricity, it was said. Jules Besinque, a former mayor of Bearcreek, and Bill Nelson were experienced machine men, and any others were expert workers in their own lines.

There was more than a 50-year range in ages among the men, from one of 19 years to one of 72.

Premonition?

Many miners will not kill a mouse inside a mine. As long as the little animals are there, it is believed to be safe. According to the old belief, when mice and insects start leaving the mine, something bad is about to happen.

John Kastelitz worked the night shift Friday night, getting off work early Saturday morning. He reported a large number of mice during his shift. "I was sitting on a parting, eating my lunch," Kastelitz reported, "and I had to move to a higher spot to get away from them."

There are those who say they were told of flies, gnats and mice making their exodus from the mine the day preceding the explosion, a sure sign of trouble ahead due to air quality problems. During research for this book, however, we found no other firsthand accounts.

Smith Mine #3 was known as "gassy," with regular reports of gas in the mine coming in for over a year before the explosion. Kastelitz also remembered seeing a lot of dust in the mine that night.

Underground springs and streams plagued Smith Mine, requiring giant pumps to operate day and night to keep water out of the tunnels. Sam Alexander no doubt voiced the thoughts of many one wintry night, thinking of water problems at the mine. Being of Scottish blood, Sam was in a group of "First Footers" making traditional visits to neighbors on New Years' Eve in a night-long celebration with solid and liquid refreshments at every turn. "We're all going to get it one of these times: caught like rats in a trap," he said to those around him in a solemn moment. Sam died with his brother miners on February 27, 1943, but not because of water, as he had expected. That poured in a little later, after the pumps were thrown out of commission when the power lines blew. One wonders now if this was a premonition with Sam, or if it was the common thought of every miner who went down the slopes daily: "Is this the day we die?"

Although coal mining was hardly a safe profession, there hadn't been a major coal mine disaster in Montana since the two fires in Red Lodge in 1906 and 1908, which claimed a total of 17 lives between them. Even in nearby Wyoming, it had been almost 20 years since the last major coal mining disaster, when 39 people had died in the explosion of Sublet #5.

Yet, old miners will hasten to say, it is a good life nevertheless, and no more dangerous than many other kinds of work. They grew to love the mines, though they knew from experience that they or their companions could be injured or die at any minute from the countless hazards always present. Most of them had seen many injuries and a good many had witnessed death among their fellow workers. Yet they continued on, finding enjoyment in their work. Life, in general, was good.

Number Three

Workers at Smith went into the mine some 8,000 feet on Seam #3. They rode the empty cars in, loaded them with coal, and sent them to the surface, pulled by electric motors. The use of animals for pulling the loads had been discontinued some years before. The tunnels of #3 ran southward from the mine entrance, up under Scotch Coulee. Today, State Highway 308 crosses over the old entrance tunnel, but the opening still shows, with some of the mine rails protruding below the highway grade.

The buildings shown on the front and back cover of this booklet are directly across the highway from the original entrance.

First Came the Wind

On the morning of February 27, 1943, hoist operator Alex Hawthorne and pump men Willard Reid and Eli Houtonen were working together in the mine. At about 9:37, they suddenly felt unusual pressure on their ears, but heard nothing. Then a terrible wind blasted at them, coming from inside the mine, carrying a load of debris with it. Hawthorne snatched up the phone, sending word out that something was wrong down in the mine, that the power was off, and that he was coming out. Then, as quickly as that, he dropped by the telephone, overcome by the methane gas (or "fire damp," as they called it).

Reid and Houtonen had started for the surface, but the wind swept them off of their feet and rolled them along the mine floor. When they stopped rolling, Reid lay face down in the middle of the tracks, gasping for any fresh air that might be left. Suddenly it became terribly quiet. Veteran miner that he was, Reid knew that the wind was coming back. He pushed his face into the ground and held his jacket around him, and he heard the wind returning.

It whistled and howled through the tunnel like a hurricane. It tore at him like a demon, and shredded the coat on his back. After it had passed, he struggled to his feet and started up the track again toward the good air outside. Then he saw Houtonen flat on the ground a few feet away, his carbide light no longer burning. Reid, whose lamp still was putting out light, prodded Houtonen to get up and get out, but Houtonen was incapacitated by the gas, too far gone to move.

"Get up!" Reid yelled. He kicked the still form on the ground, but Houtonen failed to move. Reid pulled his partner up and dragged him along, stumbling, staggering and still holding on tight. They were together like this when rescue men reached them a little later, locating Reid by his lamp.

Those battery-powered lights coming at Reid looked as big as washtubs, he said, and then he, too, passed out. He knew nothing more until he regained consciousness, deathly sick, outside the mine.

Rescuers found Dewey Hardy dead. Hawthorne was found unconscious, hanging over a rail that separated him from the tracks, and was revived in a Red Lodge hospital five miles away, where Reid and Houtonen were also kept alive. Hawthorne's son, James, was one of the 74 still in the mine.

Another miner in the hospital room with them, Ignace Marinchek, did not survive. He had reached the door on his way out, but was too weak to pull it open. He had fallen face up, overcome by the deadly gas, and did not respond to artificial respiration. Only three of the 77 men at work in the mine that day lived to tell any part of the story.

Smith Mine's electrical system, knocked out by the blast, also silenced their emergency whistles, but other mines soon blew the dread signals, spreading the word that there was trouble. Fear struck the hearts of people throughout the valley. The other mines closed down at once, and a solemn crowd of miners, families, and neighbors quickly gathered at Smith, hushed and waiting for what might come.

The Power of the Explosion

Even though the explosion couldn't be heard from the mouth of the mine, it was a gigantic blast. The Bureau of Mines report on the disaster states that 30 of the men were killed instantly by the explosion, with the remainder expiring soon thereafter.

The blast knocked a 20-ton locomotive off its tracks a quarter of a mile away from where the Federal authorities believed the explosion originated. It knocked three loaded coal cars onto their side over two-thirds of a mile away.

Supports were blown away, shafts collapsed, and debris was blown everywhere. The only external sign of the explosion was a cloud of dust and smoke coming out of the mine, and the shrilling of the disaster whistles from other area mines.

The Influx of Help

The bright sunshine of that Saturday morning grew dim, and storm clouds moved over the valley and thickened. The temperature dropped lower and lower, but few paid any attention, for the chill of mortal dread was far deeper than any of the natural kind.

Men rushed into the mine to help their comrades, found the air too bad to breathe, and staggered back out, badly harmed by the gas. Air courses had been shattered by the blast.

Temporary brattices had been set up as fast as possible to carry fresh air into the mine, but it was not until the next morning that the big fans would be repaired enough to force the clean air in. Gas masks were put into use as far as they were available. Men began to pour in from all directions as fast as vehicles could carry them. Radio news traveled fast, and before long miners from Red Lodge, Butte, Klein, Benbow and Mouat, as well as fire department personnel from Billings and miners from Salt Lake City, had reached the site to give what aid they could. Men by the score were treated in those first several hours after being overcome by fumes, before adequate equipment had come.

Gilbert Munden, young hoist operator at Mouat Mine above Dean, Montana, told years later of his experience at Smith. Word had reached that remote mountain camp quickly, and a call for volunteers brought Munden and his five Finnish co-workers to the disaster scene. Munden was something of a veteran miner himself, despite his youth, having spent many winters of his early life in Missouri coal mines before moving to Montana. He and his men were put in charge of the timbers at Smith, many of which had been blown out of place.

The first man they came to in the tunnel was an engineer with his clothes completely blown off and coal dust embedded deeply over all the surfaces of his body. A switchman had dropped between cars, and the body sat upright, wedged in position.

Munden's crew came to a new rock drop, and he had barely climbed up the ten-foot pile to examine the roof when he heard rocks moving over his head. One of the crew had followed close behind him. Munden had time only to knock the man backwards yelling, "Look Out!" when the falling rock caught him on the heels. It threw him flat and skinned him considerably from head to foot. Someone telephoned out that a man was hurt and he was carried out for emergency treatment before he rejoined his crew inside.

Side by Side

The bodies of miners were laid side by side inside the mine, as they were located, and at one time Gil Munden counted 44 in that row of canvas-wrapped bundles. All knew that families waited outside. Out of respect for them the bodies were left inside.

In one area, a man from the Bureau of Mines squeezed a fine powder from a contraption designed to test oxygen content. The normally airborne powder dropped directly to the ground rather than floating. Six bodies were found there.

Munden's crew was quickly weakened by the lack of air, but managed to load three of the bodies onto stretchers and head back out.

"You may pass out," cautioned the Bureau of Mines man, "but remember to hold on to the rope!"

Munden walked on the heels of the man in front of him and pulled at the man behind, and somehow they staggered on. "I don't think I ever fell down," he said, "but I knew when the others fell."

They got to the air, and the sudden intake of oxygen was too much for them. They were all hit with excruciating pain that threatened to split their heads wide open, and they were temporarily helpless. They dropped to the ground and waited for the pain to lessen.

"Boys," said the Bureau man, "there still are three more bodies in there we've got to get out. I want some volunteers."

Nobody spoke. Then Munden said, "Let's go!"

The Bureau man looked at him and said, "Man, you're crazy. You can't go back down there. It'd kill you." The official turned to the other men that were present. "This man is willing to go, after what he's been through. Now how about some of the rest of you?"

He got his volunteers. He sent Munden and his crew to take the three bodies they had already pulled out back to the main line. This was no small task, they found, for cave-ins had shut off passageways in places until only a squeeze-hole was left. Getting stretchers loaded with men through those places was no job for weaklings.

Other rescue workers tell of taking stretchers through water as the tunnels began to fill from the lack of pumping.

Munden said when it was finally believed that all of the hundreds of passageways had been checked, they came across a shop far, far down in the mine. The six workers therein had known their danger after the blast, and had tried desperately to barricade their area to keep out the deadly gas. They had used powder boxes and lids, dirt, rock, lunch pails: anything they could find. They had filled all but a two-foot square hole when the gas reached them. They were lying as if they had simply dropped off to sleep, but some had had time to write messages to their loved ones on powder boxes before they passed out.

"Goodbye wives and daughters. We died an easy death. Love from us both. Be good. Walter J. Johnny S." This was found beside the bodies of Walter Joki and John Sudar.

Emil Anderson left this message: "Its five min pass 11 o'clock dear Agnes and children I'm sorry we had to go this God Bless you all Emil with lots kiss."

Photo courtesy of Carbon County Historical Society

From Frank Pajnich, Fred Rasborschek, John Sudar and Walter Joki: "We try to do our best but we couldn't get out."

The Darkest Hour

Photo courtesy of Carbon County Historical Society

Gilbert Munden and his Finnish co-workers from the Mouat Mine never left the rescue work until the last body was out. Munden was sick afterwards, sicker than he likes to recall.

"I can still see the gloves," he says. "They brought them to us by the dozens of pairs — white cotton gloves — as a safety measure. After each job we had to throw them down and take a new pair for the next. Before we were through, we were walking on a carpet of white gloves."

Alex McDonald, who also helped with this story, was another who put in days of rescue work, and like the others, the experience will never leave him. Desperate attempts were made from the beginning to get to the men inside, and every man who went in before proper equipment arrived collapsed from the gas. Alex remembers two drunks who came along and bragged that they could bring those men out.

"Stay out, you two," they were told. But they blundered on in, crying out, "Oh, we can stand this!" No sooner said than the first man fell flat on his face just inside the door.

"Hey, there!" his pal said. "What's the matter?" Then he, too, fell flat. Luckily for them, others pulled them out before they were seriously hurt.

Scores of brave men tried to get to their pals inside, and all of them were overcome.

Matt Woodrow, knocked out several times by gas in repeated attempts to help, went back into the mine on Friday night to see the bodies still waiting to be brought out. There he found the remains of David Murray with the rest, and cried in anguish, "Dave! He came from the old country in the same boat with me. My pal! Now I'm living and he's dead!"

But Matt wasn't alive for long. He had inhaled too much of the noxious atmosphere of the mine, and died just a few weeks later on April 9, at age 61. He became the 75th victim of the disaster.

Help For the Living

The Red Cross, clubs, churches, sympathetic individuals — people from all sides teamed together to help the men who were doing the work inside the mine. Women set up emergency kitchens with hot coffee and food in the Cameron home in Washoe. The Red Cross promptly put "unlimited funds" at the disposal of the local group, took over the canteen, put a motor corps into action, and helped to set up an emergency hospital in Washington Hall in Red Lodge, equipped with 50 beds. A staff in their headquarters in the Meyer-Chapman bank building was on duty 24 hours per day.

The hospital was able to care for 75 patients at a time and had four trained nurses on duty. The canteen group maintained two kitchens: one at the mine and one at Washington Hall. The people and merchants donated food. High school boys were a big help in first aid work and in setting up hospital facilities. By Thursday afternoon approximately 200 people had been treated there.

The Darkest Hour

The Highway Patrol transported rescue workers to and from the mine, and took women canteen workers where they were needed, besides bringing in equipment as fast as it could be flown in from other areas. Boy Scouts served as messengers.

The State Board of Public Welfare made $10,000 available immediately, and also acquired surplus foods and garments for the families of mine victims.

The International Union of Mine Workers immediately contributed $7,400, to be distributed equally among the families of the victims. Most of the miners in Smith #3 were members. IUMW President John Lewis, along with the Vice President and Secretary-Treasurer, sent this message to Local 858 in Bearcreek:

> International officers are shocked to learn of the great tragedy that has befallen so many members of our Local Union No. 858 at Washoe. These brothers have died in the service of their country as truly as any soldier upon a remote battlefield. Our hundreds of thousands of members will grieve with the members of Local Union No. 858 and the members of the families of the deceased brothers.
>
> The international officers are placing at the disposal of President W.A. Boyle of District 27 certain funds to be used for relief purposes in this great disaster. Please convey our profound sympathy to each member of the bereaved families.

An Elks banquet planned for Saturday night in Red Lodge was cancelled, and all of the food was sent to the Bearcreek disaster site.

While squads across the entire state and beyond were coming to help, including clergymen, high mine officials, doctors and nurses, the grief-stricken families were not allowed inside the mine. They stood waiting, hoping, praying, and knowing they must expect the worst.

Top rescue teams flown in by Army planes and equipped with gas masks worked in chains, guided by local miners. A crack team of workers flown in from the Anaconda Copper Mining Company at Butte in an Army paratroop transport were able, with their good equipment, to stay in the gas-ridden mine for hours. They dug in the labyrinth of tunnels and drilled through solid rock to try to reach the men who were hedged in some 7,500 feet into the mountainside and about 800 feet down from the surface. They set up blocks against gas pockets and hunted for the injured, to rescue any that might be found living.

More than 100 local miners went in time after time, wearing filter masks, to help direct the rescue specialists who were not familiar with the complicated layout of the mine's 700 tunnels.

Governor Sam Ford of Montana went to the mine and personally offered all the assistance the State could command.

Plenty of help came quickly, indeed, but it made no difference to the 74 men inside. Their families waiting in the snow and bitter, bitter cold learned finally that their loved ones had been found beyond mortal help, and only then did they turn away.

The Grim Night Caravans

Bodies were identified by their lamp numbers and "brass checks." Some of the bodies were maimed, some were burned, and it was not until the night of Thursday, March 4th that a grim procession of trucks left the Smith Mine, carrying the mortal remains of 23 men, wrapped in brattice cloths. The procession was repeated on Friday night and again on Saturday night. The last remaining body, that of Elmer Price, was found on Sunday afternoon, eight days after the explosion. Fifty-eight women were forced to accept the fact of their widowhood.

One of them, Jean Sommerville of Washoe, lost eleven relatives in that disaster. Mary Wakenshaw lost husband, father, and father-in-law. Mrs. Clem Lodge lost husband, brother, three uncles, and several nephews. Mrs. Frank Dougherty lost ten relatives. Pete Giovetti and Mike Korinko left two of the largest families of children. Hardly a family in the valley had not suffered the loss of one or many men in the mine.

One-third of the Bearcreek School pupils were left fatherless by the calamity. Out of eight seniors, only two had fathers left alive after February 27, 1943.

There were also several workers with no known relatives.

Funeral services, multiple and single, were held daily, even before all of the bodies were found, and the snow-covered cemeteries at Bearcreek and Red Lodge were thickly dotted with new graves. Old-timers said that only once before had anywhere near so many graves been made in so short a time. That was the flu epidemic in 1918 when, in the Bearcreek cemetery alone, 24 burials took place within seven days.

A former teacher, the Rev. D. S. McCorkle of Conrad, Montana, had been a part of the Bearcreek community for ten years before 1930. He was in the Senate Chamber at Helena when news of the disaster came through. Mr. McCorkle was appearing before the Legislature in connection with the State Welfare Board, of which he was a member. He helped to remit the $10,000 grant for relief, and then rushed to the scene to be with his many old friends.

During the time he was with them, he conducted burial services for 21 individuals, and offered comfort in many ways by his presence. Solemn requiem mass for a number of victims was held in Red Lodge by the Catholic Church, with priests from Billings, Columbus and Red Lodge participating. Other churches held memorial services and some were buried with gravesite rites.

The Remarkable Families

The stoicism and courage of the families was almost unbelievable. There were practically no emotional breakdowns or hysteria during the long, painful vigil. The fortitude of the women and the children, the relatives and friends, was monumental. They faced their losses as heroically as their men had died, and began sadly to prepare, in whatever way they could, to start life on a new basis, and to learn to live with their grief.

Some of the families were still dealing with earlier deaths from the Smith Mine. Betty May Hunter (now Betty Waters) was a high school senior in 1943. She and several of her friends stood outside the mine entrance when the three survivors were brought out, and the memories of her loss came flooding back.

Ten years earlier, her father had been badly burned in Bearcreek's Foster mine. After two years of recovery, he went to work in Smith #3, and was killed in a rockfall shortly thereafter.

"Soldiers on the Home Front"

The Rev. A. W. Seebart of the Congressional Church in Billings said the 72 miners "were concerned with getting coal out for the war industry of their country. It might truly be said that they died in the service of their country."

The Aftermath

Losing 74 men in a single blast was too great a loss not to sweep others with it in its swath of destruction. Many family members became ill with pneumonia and other ailments due to the long, intensely cruel exposure and strain. Mrs. Richard Mallin, whose husband died in the mine, succumbed to a long illness a few days later. O. P. H. Shelley, Red Lodge editor and publisher of the "News," died a month after the disaster, his illness attributed directly to strain and exposure during the harrowing time. A baby died of pneumonia, the indirect result of the tragedy, and many of the rescuers never regained complete health.

Some lost fingernails and toenails and suffered from a variety of other ailments directly due to the gas. Every witness, every family member and every worker at the site of the calamity has knowledge of tragedies engendered by the disaster which would make a list far too extensive ever to be recorded in its entirety. The town of Bearcreek itself was doomed to near extinction in the years immediately following, as results of the event became more evident.

Today, cattle graze around the old mine buildings. A memorial stands at a pullout along Highway 308. Every so often, another proposal is made for opening a coal bed methane operation there, and each proposal has quietly died away.

Smith Mine's #3 slope never reopened for mining.

Placing the Blame

Nearly everyone who hears of the Smith Mine disaster for the first time asks the same question: what caused it?

It is a question that many have answered to their own satisfaction. They may be right, but an inquest held into the deaths of the miners on April 12-14 with a panel of 12 miners and Dr. John

Oleinik came up only with the official statement for the records: "Death was caused by concussion and gas."

No direct placement of blame was made by this group, although they did note that the State coal mine inspector had been there just three months earlier, and had pointed out serious safety violations. Mine officials responded that shortages of resources and manpower during wartime didn't allow them to bring the mine up to safety standards before the catastrophe.

According to a Bureau of Mines report, even though gas had been found "almost daily" by fireboss examinations, smoking was still permitted in the mine, and fuses were being used for explosives.

J. M. Freeman, general manager of the mine, and W. R. Freeman, mine superintendent, both were in California at the time of the explosion and returned home promptly.

Mine officials, in analyzing the event, found it most likely that the explosion was caused by methane, the main constituent of coal gas. Methane (CH_4), which the miners called "fire damp," is combustible like gasoline vapor. Carbon in the methane and in the coal dust, would normally unite with oxygen and the carbon burns, thus forming the poisonous carbon monoxide. This gas takes oxygen from the red blood corpuscles, thereby destroying them. The victim slowly becomes unconscious as the corpuscles are destroyed. Death is painless.

The map on the next page is from the investigation into the explosion. It shows the complexity of some of the over 700 tunnels in the Smith Mine, all of which had to be searched.

The Darkest Hour

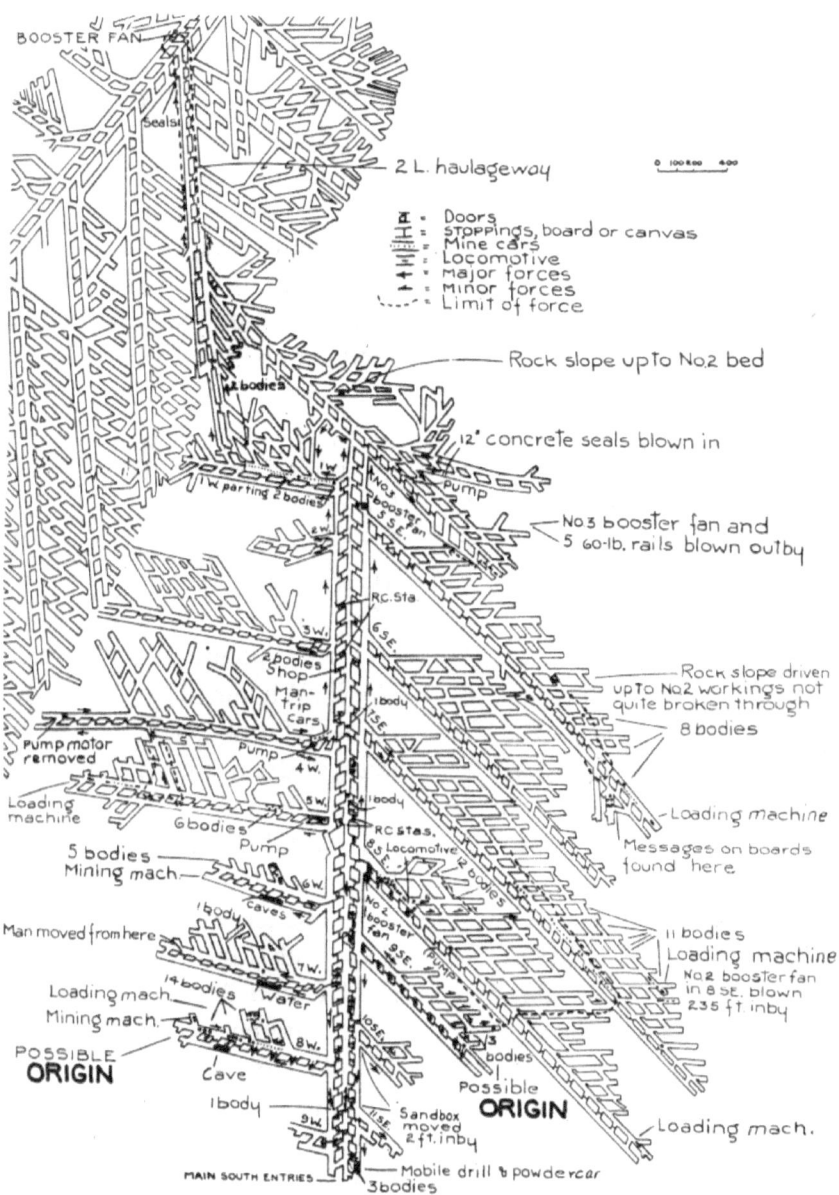

Map provided by the Carbon County Historical Society

The 74 Who Died

About half of the victims listed below lived in Bearcreek (BC) or Washoe (W), and the rest lived in Red Lodge (RL) or Roberts (R). The figure following each man's name is his age when he died. We have not been able to determine George Thompson Sr.'s age.

Alexander, Sam 57 .... BC
Allison, James 51 .... RL
Anderson, Emil 40 .... W
Appleton, Wm. Sr. 50 .... BC
Barry, William N. 26 .... RL
Barovich, Sam 56 .... BC
Besinque, Jules 51 .... BC
Beeney, William 53 .... BC
Bone, John 59 .... BC
Cline, Leland 26 .... RL
Davis, David J. 42 .... RL
DeBourg, William 55 .... RL
Deruelle, August 62 .... BC
Doran, Pat 38 .... RL
Fages, Marcel 40 .... BC
Ferro, Joe 51 .... RL
Germanetti, John 60 .... RL
Giovetti, Pete 39 .... BC
Hallila, Matt 57 .... RL
Halpin, Art 42 .... RL
Hardy, Dewey 46 .... RL
Hawthorne, James 31 .... BC
Hodnik, John 31 .... BC
Joki, Walter 30 .... RL
Jones, Wayne 31 .... RL
Jorday, Andrew 21 .... RL
Korinko, Mike 33 .... RL
Krop, John Sr. 59 .... RL
Kuhar, Louis 56 .... BC
Kumpula, Edward 35 .... RL
McDonald, Joseph 42 .... BC
McDonald, Robert 42 .... RL
McNeish, James 60 .... W
Meiklejohn, John 53 .... W
Mejean, Herman 19 .... RL
Meyer, Joe 39 .... BC
Mourich, Frank 42 .... BC
Mourich, Jack 36 .... BC
Muller, Wilbur 22 .... RL
Murray, David Sr. 56 .... BC
Mus, Earl 51 .... RL
Nelson, William 51 .... RL
Noble, William 68 .... BC
Pajnich, Frank 53 .... RL
Pelo, William 55 .... RL
Price, Elmer 53 .... RL
Pryde, William 32 .... BC
Rahkola, Zino 27 ....R
Rasborschek, Fred 61 .... BC
Ratkovich, Martin 46 .... BC
Reid, David 33 .... BC
Reid, Lawrence 41 .... BC
Saarela, George 33 .... RL
Shepard, William 69 .... W
Slaby, William 38 .... RL
Sommerville, David 60 .... W
Sommerville, John 34 .... RL
Starkovich, Frank 64 .... RL
Sudar, John 28 .... RL
Sumicek, Frank 65 .... BC

Laird, Edward 55 .... W	Thompson, George Sr. .... W
Laird, Edward J. 49 .... W	Wakenshaw, Adam 72 .... BC
Lodge, Clem 51 .... BC	Wakenshaw, Robert 39 .... BC
Madden, John 53 .... BC	Whitehead, Robert 47 .... RL
Mallin, Richard 68 .... RL	Williams, Clarence 42 .... W
Marinchek, Ignace 57 .... BC	Williams, Lloyd 45 .... W
McDonald, Abe 59 .... W	Zaputil, Vid 50 .... RL

Of the 74 miners who died that day, only seven were under 30 years of age, because so many of the area's young men were fighting in World War II.

The Smith Mine Memorial in the Bearcreek Cemetery
Photo courtesy of Durrae & John Johanek

The February 14, 1947 edition of *Bear Facts*, the newsletter from Bearcreek School, tells of the memorial stones set at last in Bearcreek and Red Lodge cemeteries. Though ordered in the fall of 1943, wartime scarcity of manpower and other difficulties delayed production.

The stones of red granite, made by Billings Monument Company, are six feet long, three feet high, and ten inches thick. They were paid for by surviving members of local miners' unions and the Montana Coal and Iron Company. The inscription, "SMITH MINE DISASTER," followed by the date, heads a three-column list of the victims.

The Children Speak

The editorial below is from Bear Facts, March 19, 1943. Betty Hunter and Marjorie Giovetti were co-editors of the school paper, and C. L. Baldwin was the advisor.

A Letter to the Servicemen

A few days ago 74 soldiers of the home front gave their lives, while producing coal to be used in the mills and factories turning out war materials. They never had a military funeral, but they were at their post on the home front when disaster struck.

It really isn't necessary to remind you of the dangers these men faced each day as they took up their post as soldiers of production here at home. Deep in our hearts we all hold a respect for these brave men who gave their all.

Three Alive

And what of the three men who survived that ordeal?

Alex Hawthorne lived almost 20 more years, dying in Billings in 1962. Eli Houtonen never regained his health. He stayed in the Bearcreek area until he died in 1964.

It was a long time until Willard Reid was healthy enough to work again. He moved to California and finally settled into a job there, returning to Montana each summer to fish, rest, visit relatives, old friends and places, and to reminisce along sparkling mountain streams. Reid received an offer to go back to work at the Smith Mine again, and considered it seriously, but his family advised against it. Reid lived for over 50 years after the calamity.

Some may wonder how he could even consider returning underground after such an experience as the Smith catastrophe. The answer is easy to those who know miners and their way of thinking. It is explained very well indeed, in another editorial written by children of miners, reproduced from *Bear Facts* below:

> **Once a Miner Always a Miner**
>
> Ignoring all thoughts of danger, most of the Bearcreek coal miners have made mining their career from way back when many of them first started down the slopes with their fathers or grandfathers. No matter what accidents have taken place or the injuries they have suffered, a miner seldom leaves this job to seek work in another line.
>
> It is in their blood. All in all, the work is not too hard, the hours not too long, the pay good enough to provide the necessities of life and a good many luxuries.

Into Hell and Back

There surely is a special place in Heaven reserved for the rescue men. They descended into unimaginable conditions for their comrades. They lived with an overpowering presence of death, monstrously magnified, as they worked in those dank, dark tunnels of horror, knowing that any second the mine could blow again, blasting them, also, into bits. They knew at any second that more rock could drop, burying them under thousands of tons of rock forever. They knew that gas pockets could open any second from one of those hundreds of black passageways and snuff them out as it had the others.

Yet they labored doggedly on, hour after weary hour, day after day, too sickened by what they found to relish food; too saturated with the presence of death to coddle their own bodies. Here was an agonizing job to be done. Those families waiting outside needed those mortal remains of their loved ones for that last bit of comfort afforded by decent burial: the formal, final commitment of their religious faith.

Those rescue men cannot forget what they found and what they experienced. They carry lifetime memories with them of that time when the little towns of Bearcreek and Washoe were forced into Treasure State history as the scene of the worst coal mining disaster that Montana had ever known.

The Darkest Hour

The Worst Coal Mining Disasters

As we've said elsewhere in this booklet, the Smith Mine #3 explosion was the worst coal-mining disaster in Montana's history, and its second-worst mining disaster of any kind following the fire in Butte's Granite Mountain copper mine in 1917, which took 163 lives.

What follows is a list of the 50 worst coal mining incidents in United States history, according to the National Institute for Occupational Safety and Health (NIOSH) as of July 2010 (Smith Mine #3 is 43rd on the list):

Rank	Year	Mine	Location	Deaths
1	1907	Monongah No. 6 and 8	Monongah, WV	362
2	1913	Stag Canon No. 2	Dawson, NM	263
3	1909	Cherry	Cherry, IL	259
4	1907	Darr	Jacobs Creek, PA	239
5	1900	Winter Quarters 1 & 4	Scofield, UT	200
6	1928	Mather No. 1	Mather, PA	195
7	1902	Fraterville	Coal Creek, TN	184
8	1914	Eccles No. 5 & No. 6	Eccles, WV	181
9	1904	Harwick	Cheswick, PA	179
10	1924	No. 2	Castle Gate, UT	172
11	1903	Hanna, No. 1	Hanna, WY	169
12	1908	Rachel and Agnes	Marianna, PA	154
13	1911	Banner	Littleton, AL	128
14	1972	Buffalo Mining Co.	Saunders, WV	125
15	1917	Hastings	Hastings, CO	121
16	1923	Stag Canon No. 1	Dawson, MN	120
17	1924	Benwood	Benwood, WV	119
18	1951	Orient No. 2	West Frankfort, IL	119
19	1915	Layland No. 3	Layland, WV	115
20	1902	Rolling Mill	Johnstown, PA	112
21	1905	Virginia City	Virginia City, AL	112
22	1884	Laurel	Pocahontas, VA	112
23	1947	No. 5	Centralia, IL	111

Rank	Year	Mine	Location	Deaths
24	1869	Avondale	Plymouth, PA	110
25	1891	Mammouth	Mount Pleasant, PA	109
26	1892	No. 11	Krebs, OK	100
27	1923	Frontier No. 1	Kemmerer, WY	99
28	1913	Cincinnati	Finleyville, PA	98
29	1927	Federal No. 3	Everettville, WV	97
30	1919	Baltimore Tunnel #2	Wilkes-Barre, PA	92
31	1926	No. 21	Wilburton, OK	91
32	1940	Pond Creek No. 1	Bartley, WV	91
33	1922	Dolomite No. 3	Dolomite, AL	90
34	1907	Stuart	Stuart, WV	84
35	1910	Palos No. 3	Palos, AL	84
36	1911	Cross Mountain	Briceville, TN	84
37	1930	No. 6	Millfield, OH	82
38	1912	Jed	Jed, WV	81
39	1910	Victor American No. 3	Delagua, CO	79
40	1922	Reilly No. 1	Spangler, PA	79
41	1968	Consol No. 9	Farmington, WV	78
42	1910	Primero	Primero, CO	75
43	*1943*	*Smith No. 3*	*Washoe, MT*	*74*
44	1911	Price-Pancoast	Troop, PA	73
45	1912	San Bois No. 2	McCurtain, OK	73
46	1940	Willow Grove No. 10	St. Clairsville, OH	72
47	1883	Diamond	Braidwood, IL	69
48	1867	Bright Hope	Winterpock, VA	69
49	1909	Lick Branch	Switchback, WV	67
50	1944	Powhatan	Powhatan Point, OH	66

Of these 50 tragedies, 44 of them have the same listed cause as the Smith disaster: explosions.

Note also that only five of the disasters on the list happened after 1943. Why is that? Certainly there are fewer people working in coal mines today (114,458 in 2001 compared with 486,516 in 1943), but improved mine safety is another major factor. In 1943, one out of every 335 coal mine workers died on the job. In 2001, it was one out of every 2725: an eight-fold improvement.

These safety improvements came too late for the men who died in the Smith Mine in 1943. Each mining death, however, provided greater impetus to solve the underlying problems. The report showing that gas had been regularly found in Smith, along with open-flame lamps and inadequately protected high-voltage lines, stimulated development of stiffer safety regulations.

Each of the men who died that day became another driving force for improved mine safety. The contributions of these miners continue, even after their deaths.

Hauling coal from a Bearcreek area mine.
Photo courtesy of Carbon County Historical Society

Epilogue

And there it is, the story of the darkest hour of Carbon County's history—a disaster ranked as the 35th worst in the nation's coal mining tragedies to that time and the 43rd worst ever as of this 3rd edition of 2010.

Many of the men had been leaders in their community: men of stature and ability far beyond the requirements of their daily jobs in the mine. The heritage they left was also great, in the example of their lives, in the generation of children they had sired and loved, children taught how to be strong, and how to face disaster without losing control of their lives.

By these tokens, and through the hearts and memories of the many who cherished these brave men, the world was made better because they lived, and their work, indeed, had been well done.

www.ingramcontent.com/pod-product-compliance
Lightning Source LLC
Chambersburg PA
CBHW020628300426
44112CB00010B/1247